ANOTHER POEM HE'LL NEVER READ

By
Amber Moss

© 2024 by Amber Moss

Also by Amber Moss

Poems He'll Never Read

Thanatophobia

Some Kind of Black

To Her

Bucket of Thorns

CONTENTS

Part I: The First 30 Days   5
Part II: When the Teardrops Stop Falling   37

PART I

The First 30 Days

Wednesday 7:27 PM

This is really hard.

What is?

Pulling away.

Yes. I suppose it is.

—

Day 1 Without You

It's the quiet aftermath and
the memories of you and I
begin to slip through my fingers.

It's like trying to catch smoke

a unique kind of pain,

a mixture of mourning and
acceptance.

I want to wish you solace
and peace in the days to come.

But I can't.

I don't want to love you.
I don't want to stare at your empty side of the closet
each morning.
I don't want to feel my coffee go cold and
know you aren't there to refill my cup.

I
    don't
        want
            to
                love
                    you.

But I still do...

I reached for my phone this morning
knowing there wouldn't be a

good morning.

Day 5 Without You

It's Thanksgiving.

My sheets are fluffier on your side of the bed
and no longer match your contour.

I imagine we have a family of our own
and our kids dance around the fireplace
while we glaze a ham together.

Then I snap out of it.

Tell me you haven't forgotten about me yet.

I FEEL SO ALONE
I FEEL SO ALONE
I FEEL SO ALONE
I FEEL SO ALONE
I FEEL SO ALONE
I FEEL SO ALONE
I FEEL SO ALONE
I FEEL SO ALONE

I never thought I'd forget how to exist
without you.

I keep coming back to this image of
you and I in the theater
smiling at the same time.

Day 10 Without You

They say that grief is the most intense emotion after a breakup, but I feel confusion. If you said you didn't want to be without me,

why did you leave?

I hope I'm still your favorite person.

My idea of love has been deteriorated
like wood beneath termites

as I helped you float
while I drowned.

I stare at her photo
wondering how the pieces fit
and I imagine you together
laughing at jokes I don't understand.

I wanted a love that consumed me.

But no one told me how bad it would hurt.

Day 15 Without You

I'm exhausted from missing you.
Exhausted from moving in the dark without you.
Exhausted from forcing smiles in front of strangers.

Exhausted....

My friends told me I dance beautifully on my own.

There's a love letter addressed to you that I never
sent.

I'm ~~not~~ angry.
I'm ~~not~~ angry.
I'm ~~not~~ angry.
I'm ~~not~~ angry.
I'm ~~not~~ angry.
I'm ~~not~~ angry.
I'm ~~not~~ angry.
I'm ~~not~~ angry.
I'm ~~not~~ angry.
I'm ~~not~~ angry.
I'm ~~not~~ angry.
I'm ~~not~~ angry.
I'm ~~not~~ angry.
I'm ~~not~~ angry.
I'm ~~not~~ angry.
I'm ~~not~~ angry.

My heart still craves you.

A craving that intensifies with time
in an attempt to give my heartbreak a voice
even if it's a silent one.

Day 20 Without You

The wind is colder and the ground freezes
beneath my feet.

The flowers have wilted and left stories
of both pain and love,
and I begin to pluck what's left of the petals
wondering if they feel agony like I do.

How pitiful is it
to long for someone
who can't even love you?

Do you hurt as much as I do
when the sun goes down?

Hearts beat fast
but lessons are learned slowly.

I'm ~~not~~ over you.
I'm ~~not~~ over you.
I'm ~~not~~ over you.
I'm ~~not~~ over you.
I'm ~~not~~ over you.
I'm ~~not~~ over you.

Day 25 Without You

I burned the skirt I wore on our first date.
Ivory and sage dance in the flames
while sticks cackle and break.

Just like me.

I shift whiskey in a glass
until your face is distorted in my mind.

I read your heart wrong
because I thought I knew
its language.

Shamefully,
I still think about our future together.

I posted a new photo
hoping you'd notice.

Day 30 Without You

I imagine the day I see you again
there will be laughter and old tales
of how you broke the woman that
kept you together.

PART 2

When the Teardrops Stop Falling

There's a quote that says,

The only thing we never get enough of, is love...

So, if you choose to love yourself, you will always be enough.

Isaiah's Poem

Betrayal seemed easy
as if you are in tuned with it

A dance that only you could master,
so intricate and beautiful

I almost forgot how to cry.

You built him up
while he broke you down.

Climb up without him.

You gave kindness and didn't get kindness back.
It doesn't make you a fool.
It makes you resilient.

Acceptance is quite a revolution within oneself.

Our love story began quietly,
so quiet that I didn't notice when it even began.

It ended loudly.

Intervention

I like to hold onto memories,
keep old photos saved in my phone
and act surprised
when they pop up on my loneliest days.

My friends say I get off
on torture
because only I would slice
my own heart and display it
on my nightstand.

I know that he was your source of comfort,
like tomato soup on a cold afternoon
and warmth in your veins.

But I want you to find comfort
in silence.
The snowfall outside your window.
The sun rising just as you've opened your eyes.
Peace in knowing he's not there to hurt you again.

You can't unlove him
but you can love him from a distance.

I've been practicing patience.

Unclenching my jaw during moments of uncertainty.

Driving past our favorite places until it doesn't hurt anymore.

Breathing...

When I needed you to breathe,
you let me suffocate.

Your heart will beat without him
the rhythm will just be different.

Petals fall and you don't catch them
because what was once a signal of love
has become a signal of breaking and longing.

The heart never runs out of space
it just expands for new love.

Kason's Poem

You admit being lonely
in the cozy place you made yours
shoes undone in the middle of the floor.
Outside, the lights grow dim while an alley cat
wails near the window.

I think you would love the nearest person to you
if they were foolish enough,
cling to you at 3 am
when the only people awake are
the isolated and disguised
in downtown bars and wrecked streets.

Some people only want to see your scars
so they know where you bleed.

Before you go back,
remember how you lit fires
just to feel something.

Smile.

Even when you want to cry.

What Does Your Heart Need?

A cheerful playlist / a hammock on a tropical island where time forgets to tick / a warm cup of moonlight tea / a whisper from tomorrow / a cozy corner / a bouquet of flowers / love...

And sometimes there's not enough time
to heal every wound,
but there is enough time
to love someone new.

I know it seems maniacal
delivering words of love and loss
on pen and paper
then soaking it in wine
in the hours after the sun has settled
behind the trees.

Johnathan's Poem

When they ask me,

What's the best thing that's ever happened to you?

I'll say your name.

When they ask me,

What's the worst thing that's ever happened to you?

I'll say your name.

This is the last poem I'll write about you.

The tears have stopped falling, but I know it's still hard. I know it's hard to wake up and wish this were the day you stopped loving him. I know it's hard to go to bed and see their face in your dreams. I know it's hard to finally give up hope of them learning to love you the way that you deserve. You feel sick and exhausted. You want to feel joy in a world that profits off pain. And someday you will. Be brave enough to love again.

It's time to dance like your feet remember the
freedom of a child's laughter.

Say Farewell

Memories linger and each moment shared
will eventually fall
into a silent spell.

So here we stand,
voices low,
hearts broken,
ready to turn the page
and say farewell.

FAREWELL.

About Amber Moss

Amber Moss is a poet in Atlanta, GA. She received her undergraduate degree in English from the University of South Florida and her graduate degree in Marketing from LIM College. She is the author of three poetry chapbooks and three full-length poetry collections. She is devoted to helping her generation feel comfortable in their individuality through poetry. Amber's work touches on love, loss, trauma, culture, and sexuality.

Her individual poems can be found on ambermoss.org.

www.ingramcontent.com/pod-product-compliance
Lightning Source LLC
Chambersburg PA
CBHW021349160726
47994CB00007B/2890